My United States

Alaska

JOSH GREGORY

Children's Press®
An Imprint of Scholastic Inc.

Content Consultant

James Wolfinger, PhD, Associate Dean and Professor
College of Education, DePaul University, Chicago, Illinois

Library of Congress Cataloging-in-Publication Data
Names: Gregory, Josh, author.
Title: Alaska / by Josh Gregory.
Description: New York, NY : Children's Press, 2017. | Series: A true book | Includes bibliographical references and index.
Identifiers: LCCN 2016057536| ISBN 9780531252512 (library binding : alk. paper) | ISBN 9780531232811 (pbk. : alk. paper)
Subjects: LCSH: Alaska—Juvenile literature.
Classification: LCC F904.3 .G73 2017 | DDC 979.8—dc23
LC record available at https://lccn.loc.gov/2016057536

Photographs ©: cover: Kenneth Whitten/Media Bakery; back cover ribbon: AliceLiddelle/Getty Images; back cover bottom: Josh Miller Photography/Getty Images; 3 bottom: Kokkai Ng/iStockphoto; 3 map: Jim McMahon; 4 left: zokru/Thinkstock; 4 right: tr3gi/Thinkstock; 5 bottom: benoitrousseau/Getty Images; 5 top: Alaska Stock/Superstock, Inc.; 7 center bottom: Eric Baccega/Nature Picture Library; 7 top: Gabriel Johnson/Shutterstock; 7 center top: Steven Kazlowski/age fotostock; 7 bottom: Design Pics Inc/Alamy Images; 8-9: davidhoffmannphotography/iStockphoto; 11: Grant Dixon/Getty Images; 12: Kevin Smith/Getty Images; 13: Eric Engman/Fairbanks Daily News-Miner/AP Images; 14 top: Doug Lindstrand/Newscom; 14 bottom: Tuned_In/Getty Images; 15: Donald M. Jones/Minden Pictures; 16-17: SteveChristensen/iStockphoto; 19: James Poulson/The Daily Sitka Sentinel/AP Images; 20: Tigatelu/iStockphoto; 22 right: Carsten Reisinger/Shutterstock; 22 left: Uvex/Vector-Images.com; 23 center right: tr3gi/Thinkstock; 23 top left: VvoeVale/Thinkstock; 23 bottom right: benoitrousseau/Getty Images; 23 bottom left: Milo Burcham/Design Pics/Getty Images; 23 center left: zokru/Thinkstock; 23 top right: Arterra/Getty Images; 24-25: AF archive/Alamy Images; 26: Vitus Bering and Alexei Chirikov in Petropavlovsk, 1989 (oil on cardboard), Pshenichny, Igor Pavlovich (b.1938)/State Central Navy Museum, St. Petersburg/Bridgeman Art Library; 27 bottom left: SteveChristensen/iStockphoto; 27 top right: Uvex/Vector-Images.com; 27 top left: Universal History Archive/Getty Images; 27 bottom right: AP Images; 29: Vitus Bering and Alexei Chirikov in Petropavlovsk, 1989 (oil on cardboard), Pshenichny, Igor Pavlovich (b.1938)/State Central Navy Museum, St. Petersburg/Bridgeman Art Library; 30: String of fox furs, Alaska, USA (b/w photo), Hutchison, I. W. (19th century)/Royal Geographical Society, London, UK/Bridgeman Art Library; 31: Brady National Photographic Art Gallery (Washington, D.C.)Library of Congress; 32: Universal History Archive/Getty Images; 34-35: Alaska Stock/age fotostock; 36: Jeff Schultz/Media Bakery; 37: Al Grillo/AP Images; 38: Alaska Stock/Superstock, Inc.; 39: Alaska Stock; 40 inset: Al Grillo/AP Images; 40 bottom: PepitoPhotos/iStockphoto; 41: Alaska Stock/Superstock, Inc.; 42 top left: ASL-P20-012/Alaska State Library; 42 top right: ASL-P01-3294/Alaska State Library; 42 bottom left: ASL-P14-066/Alaska State Library; 42 bottom right: AP Images; 43 top left: R. Diamond/Getty Images; 43 top right: Noel Vasquez/Getty Images; 43 bottom left: Adam Nadel/AP Images; 43 bottom right: Noel Vasquez/Getty Images; 44 top: Design Pics Inc/Alamy Images; 44 center: grafxart8888/iStockphoto; 44 bottom left: Gabriel Bouys/Getty Images; 44 bottom right: stanley45/iStockphoto; 45 top left: AP Images; 45 top right: Mickrick/iStockphoto; 45 center: stanley45/iStockphoto; 45 bottom: Eric Engman/Fairbanks Daily News-Miner/AP Images.

Maps by Map Hero, Inc.

SCHOLASTIC, CHILDREN'S PRESS, A TRUE BOOK™, and associated logos are trademarks and/or registered trademarks of Scholastic Inc., 557 Broadway, New York, NY 10012.

1 2 3 4 5 6 7 8 9 10 R 27 26 25 24 23 22 21 20 19 18

Front cover: A brown bear fishing for salmon in Katmai National Park

Back cover: A bald eagle

Welcome to Alaska

Find the Truth!

Everything you are about to read is true **except** for one of the sentences on this page.

Which one is **TRUE**?

T or F The United States purchased Alaska from Great Britain in 1867.

T or F There are parts of Alaska where the sun doesn't rise for up to 10 weeks at a time.

Find the answers in this book.

Contents

THE **BIG** TRUTH!

Forget-me-not

What Represents Alaska?

Moose

A fishing boat off the coast of Alaska

Alaska's state sport
is dog mushing.

This Is Alaska!

UTQIAGVIK (BARROW)

1

2

BEAUFORT SEA

Colville

Brooks Range

Arctic National Wildlife Refuge

RUSSIA

BERING STRAIT

3

Denali

Gold Rush Town

Yukon

CANADA

NOME

ALASKA

FAIRBANKS

Tanana

Iditarod

Alaska Native Heritage Center

Klondike Gold Rush National Historical Park

Alaska St Capito

Alaska Zoo

BERING SEA

ANCHORAGE

VALDEZ

SKAGWAY

Lake Iliamna

JUNEAU

The Valley of Ten Thousand Smokes

BRISTOL BAY

SEWARD

SITKA

Alaska SeaLife Center

KODIAK

Sitka National Historical Park

Aleutian Islands

GULF OF ALASKA

UNALASKA

4

PACIFIC OCEAN

Aleutian Islands

UNALASKA

0   200
Miles

6

1 Utqiagvik

Utqiagvik (formerly Barrow), Alaska, is the United States' most northerly city. Far north of the **Arctic Circle**, Utqiagvik can go up to 10 weeks at a time without any sunlight. Keep an eye on the sky for a chance to see the aurora borealis, or northern lights.

2 Arctic National Wildlife Refuge

At more than 19.6 million acres (7.9 million hectares), this is the National Wildlife Refuge System's largest wilderness area. The refuge was created in 1960 to protect the land, water, plants, and wildlife.

3 Denali National Park and Preserve

Located in south-central Alaska, this national park covers roughly 6 million acres (2.4 million ha). Visitors can experience **tundra**, forests, glaciers, and mountains, and see a range of wildlife.

4 Aleutian Islands

This string of 14 large islands and more than 50 smaller ones extends from the Alaska **Peninsula**. Parts of the Aleutian Islands are home to several Native Alaskan communities. Other areas are perfect for hiking, fishing, or wildlife viewing.

Alaska contains more than 3 million lakes and 40 percent of all the surface water in the United States.

CHAPTER 1

Land and Wildlife

Everything about Alaska seems gigantic! Its **territory** is nearly one-fifth the size of all the other states combined. Denali, its highest point, is the tallest mountain in North America. There's even a glacier in Alaska that's larger than Rhode Island!

The name "Alaska" comes from a local native word meaning "the great land." And its famous nickname, the Last **Frontier,** hints at Alaska's vast and dramatic wilderness.

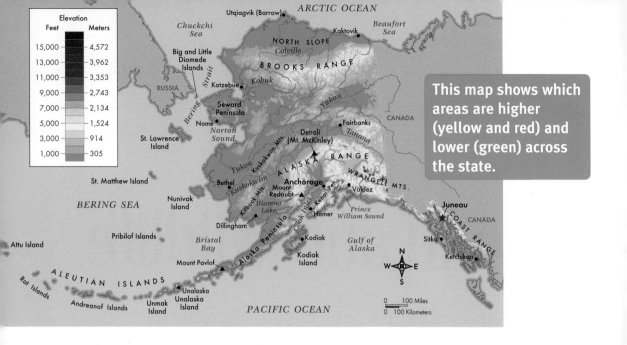

This map shows which areas are higher (yellow and red) and lower (green) across the state.

A Scenic State

Alaska is famous for its natural beauty. Traveling across the state, you'll see towering mountain peaks and active volcanoes. You'll also encounter wide-open stretches of frozen tundra, where no trees grow and the ground is **permafrost**. In other areas, there are dense forests and swampy wetlands. Along the coast, you can glimpse floating icebergs. They broke off of sheets of ice called glaciers, which cover huge areas of land.

A Mighty Mountain

The mountain named Denali is Alaska's tallest peak. In fact, with a height of 20,310 feet (6,190 meters), it is the highest point in all of North America. For many years, Denali was known as Mount McKinley. It was named after President William McKinley in 1897. In 2015, however, its original Native Alaskan name was restored. As the main attraction of Denali National Park and Preserve, this incredible mountain draws many visitors to the state.

Don't Forget Your Coat

With about one-third of the state located above the Arctic Circle, Alaska can be a very cold place. Temperatures below 0 degrees Fahrenheit (−18 degrees Celsius) are common. Strong winds can make it feel even colder. However, the weather isn't always chilly in Alaska. In some parts of the state, such as the south and southeast, summers can be warm and pleasant. This is where most Alaskans live.

MAXIMUM
TEMPERATURE
100°F

MINIMUM
TEMPERATURE
-80°F

Snowmobiles, also called snow machines, are often used in areas with no roads.

Daylight and Darkness

The most northerly parts of Alaska are close to the North Pole. During winter, this part of the planet tilts away from the sun. In the far north, Alaskans experience up to 67 days in a row with no sunlight. During summer, the North Pole tilts toward the sun. This can cause up to 80 straight days when the sun does not set. Even at night, the sun shines. Because of this, Alaska is sometimes called the Land of the Midnight Sun.

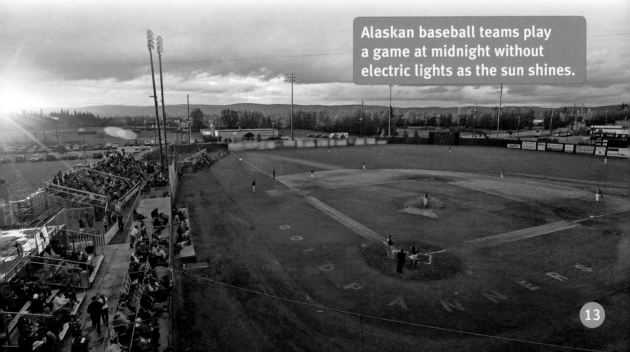

Alaskan baseball teams play a game at midnight without electric lights as the sun shines.

A pine grosbeak feeds on mountain ash berries in Anchorage.

Plants in the Permafrost

Tundra covers about half of Alaska. Much of the tundra is located to the west and north and high in mountains. Trees and other tall plants cannot survive here. Instead, a range of bushes, wildflowers, and other plants grow close to the ground. Wild berries grow in many places. In contrast to the tundra, about one-quarter of the state is forested. Here, you'll see a variety of trees. Evergreens such as spruce and cedar are especially common.

Fireweed blossom

Alaska's Animals

Many animals live in Alaska's rugged wilderness. Huge brown and grizzly bears live in the interior, while polar bears inhabit the far north. Moose, caribou, and wolves are common. Thick fur helps these mammals survive the harsh Alaskan winter. Marine mammals such as seals, otters, walruses, and whales can be spotted along the coast. These animals have layers of fat called blubber that keep them warm in the cold ocean waters.

Unlike other deer, both male and female caribou have antlers.

Juneau was made the territorial capital in 1900 and the seat of Alaska's government in 1906.

CHAPTER 2

Government

Alaska's capital city is Juneau, far to the southeast in the "panhandle" region of the state. Juneau is isolated from other Alaskan towns. There are no roads leading into the city! The only way to get there is to fly or ride a ferry. Despite the capital's remote location, it plays a central role in Alaskan life. This is where the state's leaders gather to create new laws and make important decisions about the state's future.

State Government Basics

Alaska's state government is divided into three branches. The executive branch, led by the governor, carries out the state's laws. The legislative branch writes the laws. The state's Senate and House of Representatives form this branch. Alaska's courts make up the judicial branch. The highest court is the Supreme Court. Its five justices meet at various times in Anchorage, Fairbanks, Juneau, and sometimes other communities. This lets them hear cases where the original trials took place.

ALASKA'S STATE GOVERNMENT

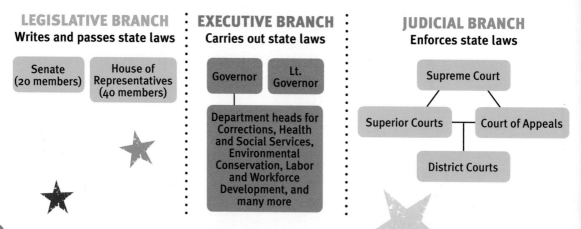

LEGISLATIVE BRANCH
Writes and passes state laws

Senate (20 members)

House of Representatives (40 members)

EXECUTIVE BRANCH
Carries out state laws

Governor

Lt. Governor

Department heads for Corrections, Health and Social Services, Environmental Conservation, Labor and Workforce Development, and many more

JUDICIAL BRANCH
Enforces state laws

Supreme Court

Superior Courts

Court of Appeals

District Courts

Members of a native corporation wear traditional clothing during a meeting in Sitka.

Alaska is divided into units called boroughs. These boroughs cover only about one-third of the state. The remaining two-thirds of the state have few residents and aren't divided into political units.

Alaska also includes regional and village native corporations. These are businesses that function much like independent tribal governments elsewhere in the country. The corporations control 44 million acres (17.8 ha) of land. They work to provide money and land to Native Alaskans.

Alaska in the National Government

Each state elects officials to represent it in the U.S. Congress. Like every state, Alaska has two senators. The U.S. House of Representatives relies on a state's population to determine its numbers. With few residents, Alaska has only one representative in the House.

Every four years, states vote on the next U.S. president. Each state is granted a number of electoral votes based on its members in Congress. With two senators and one representative, Alaska has three electoral votes.

2 senators and 1 representative

3 electoral votes

With its small population, Alaska plays only a small part in presidential elections.

Representing Alaska

Elected officials in Alaska represent a population
with a range of interests, lifestyles, and backgrounds.

Ethnicity (2015 estimates)

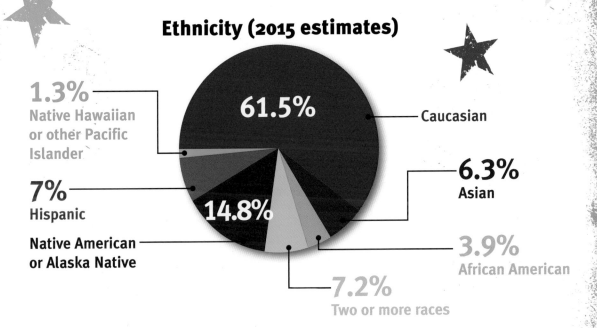

1.3%
Native Hawaiian
or other Pacific
Islander

61.5% Caucasian

6.3%
Asian

7%
Hispanic

14.8%

Native American
or Alaska Native

3.9%
African American

7.2%
Two or more races

7%
of Alaskans were born
in other countries.

63% own their
own homes.

2/3 live in
cities.

16% of the state's
citizens speak a
language other
than English at
home.

92% of the population graduated
from high school.

28% have higher
degrees.

What Represents Alaska?

States choose specific animals, plants, and objects to represent the values and characteristics of the land and its people. Find out why these symbols were chosen to represent Alaska or discover surprising curiosities about them.

Seal

Alaska's state seal was designed in 1910. Its snowy mountains, ocean water, and other features were chosen to show the beauty of Alaska's landscape.

Flag

Thirteen-year-old Benny Benson won a contest to design Alaska's state flag in 1927, when Alaska was still a territory. The background is blue, for Alaska's sky and its state flower, the forget-me-not. On this backdrop are the Great Bear constellation, representing strength, and the North Star, which stands for Alaska's future and position as the northernmost state.

Jade

STATE GEMSTONE

Large amounts of this green gemstone can be found underground and within Alaska's mountains.

Four Spot Skimmer Dragonfly

STATE INSECT

This dragonfly was chosen as the state insect by Alaskan schoolchildren in 1995.

Moose

STATE LAND MAMMAL

The largest deer in the world, these enormous creatures can be found throughout much of Alaska.

Forget-Me-Not

STATE FLOWER

These beautiful flowers grow high up in Alaska's mountainside meadows.

Willow Ptarmigan

STATE BIRD

This bird's feathers are white during winter, but change to brown in warmer weather.

Dog Mushing

STATE SPORT

Once a common form of transportation in Alaska, dog mushing has become a very popular sport.

Dogsledding developed among native groups in Alaska and Canada and is still used today.

Ethan Hawke and Klaus Maria Brandauer, *White Fang* (1991)

CHAPTER 3

History

Thousands of years ago, the sea level around the world was much lower than it is today. As a result, land between Asia and Alaska, which is now under the body of water called the Bering Strait, was exposed. People were able to simply walk from what is now eastern Russia into what has become Alaska. In about 10,000 BCE, the first people to come to Alaska crossed this now-vanished land bridge.

Paleo-Indians

The prehistoric people who first settled Alaska are known as Paleo-Indians. They survived mainly by hunting Alaska's many animals. In addition to bears, whales, and other animals still living today, they hunted the enormous and now-extinct woolly mammoth. The furs of these animals helped keep the Paleo-Indians warm in their icy new home. People used the animals' bones to make weapons and tools, and their skins to build boats.

Timeline of Alaska Events

10,000 BCE
People come to Alaska for the first time.

1741 CE
The first outside settlers arrive in Alaska.

1867
The United States purchases Alaska from Russia for $7.2 million.

10,000 BCE › 1741 CE › 1784 › 1867

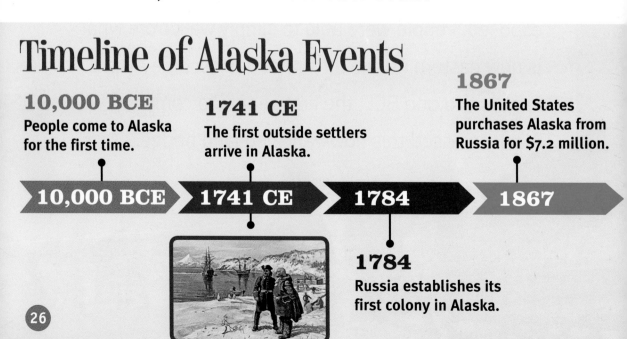

1784
Russia establishes its first colony in Alaska.

Developing Cultures

Over time, the Paleo-Indians separated into different groups. They spread across the land that would become Alaska and developed unique cultures.

For example, the Athabascans have traditionally lived in Alaska's interior near waterways where they could fish. They moved from place to place often and traveled using boats and dogsleds. The Aleuts lived along Alaska's southwestern peninsula and on the nearby Aleutian Islands. They fished from boats.

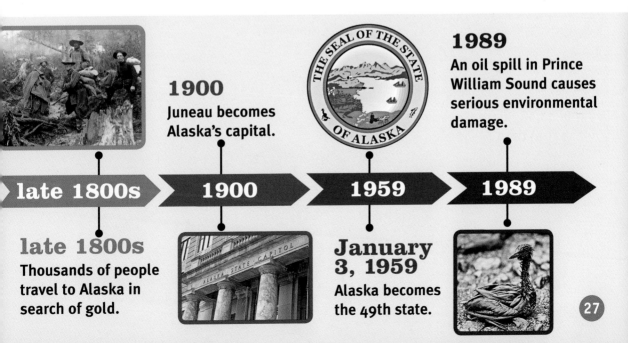

1989
An oil spill in Prince William Sound causes serious environmental damage.

1900
Juneau becomes Alaska's capital.

THE SEAL OF THE STATE OF ALASKA

late 1800s

1900

1959

1989

late 1800s
Thousands of people travel to Alaska in search of gold.

January 3, 1959
Alaska becomes the 49th state.

The Inupiats lived mainly in the northern and northwestern parts of Alaska. The Yup'iks were found in the southwest, where they rarely stayed in one place, moving constantly as they tracked their prey. The Tlingits lived in the southeastern panhandle, while the Haidas lived nearby on Prince of Wales Island.

These and other native cultures still survive in Alaska today.

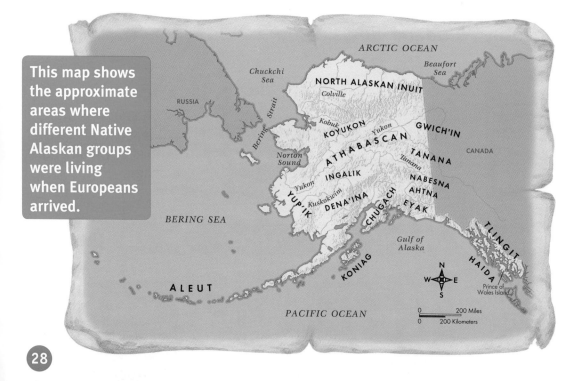

This map shows the approximate areas where different Native Alaskan groups were living when Europeans arrived.

Vitus Bering (left) stands on the shores of Alaska.

Visitors From the West

In 1741, Russian naval officer Vitus Bering sailed east across the sea from Russia in search of new lands. He and his men landed in Alaska and found a bounty of valuable animals and other natural resources. Soon, ships were regularly traveling back and forth from Russia to collect furs and other goods from Alaska to sell. The Russians often clashed with the Native Alaskans and even forced the Aleuts to help them hunt local animals.

Alaska and America

Russia controlled Alaska for many decades. But in the early 1800s, British and American fur trappers began moving into the region. At first, these three nations signed a **treaty** agreeing to share Alaska. Russia and Great Britain agreed on a border, now the Alaska-Canada border, between Russian and British lands in 1825. Over time, the fur trade became less profitable. In 1867, the United States offered to purchase Alaska for $7.2 million, which is approximately $120 million in today's money.

William Seward

The main person behind the Alaska purchase was U.S. Secretary of State William Seward. Seward believed the land would be a valuable source of supplies for the United States. He knew it was bursting with wood, fish, and a variety of **minerals**. With the fur trade slowing down, however, many Americans did not see the value of the purchase. "Seward's Folly" became a popular nickname for the new territory. Alaska, however, soon proved these people wrong.

Top hats and canes were common attire for many Americans in the 1800s.

The 49th State

Beginning in 1861, yet another valuable resource was discovered in Alaska—gold! In a rush to get rich from this new discovery, tens of thousands of people flowed into the state. Some searched for gold, while others established businesses to serve them. Towns and cities sprang up, and railroads were built to make travel across the state easier. By 1900, Alaska's population had doubled to more than 63,000 people.

The Gold Rush brought thousands of men to Alaska with the dream of becoming rich. Many of them died in the effort.

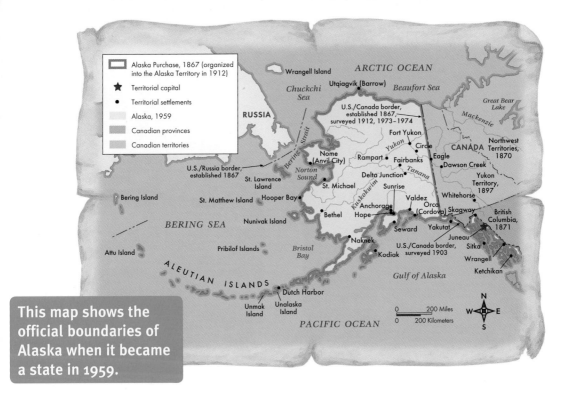

This map shows the official boundaries of Alaska when it became a state in 1959.

On January 3, 1959, Alaska officially became the 49th state. In the following decade, people discovered huge amounts of oil underground. This led to another economic boom as businesses rushed to build oil wells and pipelines. Many jobs were created, and more new residents poured into the state. Oil remains a driving force in the economy, though some people worry about drilling, transportation, and possible spills harming the environment.

Ice fishers cut a hole through the frozen surface of a body of water to catch fish.

CHAPTER 4

Culture

Alaskan culture is a blend of influences from Native Alaskans and the many people who have come to the state more recently. For example, Native Alaskan music is very popular in the state, and many musicians combine traditional sounds with more modern styles. The state's rugged landscape is another influence on its culture. Writers such as Jack London have told many tales of adventure set in the Alaskan wilderness.

The Iditarod has been held every year since 1973.

More than 1,000 dogs participate in each Iditarod race.

Sports in the Snow

While Alaskans enjoy popular sports such as baseball and hockey, the state is also home to events you won't find anywhere else in the country. Alaska's state sport is dog mushing, or dogsled racing. The annual Iditarod Trail Sled Dog Race is the state's biggest sporting event. It draws fans and competitors from around the world. The 1,100-mile (1,770 km) race winds through the Alaskan wilderness and takes up to two weeks to finish.

Time to Celebrate

Alaskans enjoy many celebrations and traditions that are unique to their state. Each July, the state hosts the World Eskimo-Indian Olympics, where Native Alaskan athletes compete in a variety of events based on traditional Alaskan survival skills. On October 18, Alaskans celebrate Alaska Day, a holiday that marks the anniversary of the state's transfer from Russia to the United States.

An athlete is flung into the air using a blanket at the World Eskimo-Indian Olympics.

Fishers haul in a net full of salmon off the coast of Alaska.

Alaska fishers often spend two to three months at sea without a break.

Alaskans at Work

As it always has been, Alaska's economy is driven by the state's wealth of natural resources. Many people are employed in the oil industry. Others work for mining companies. The state's many mines produce metals such as gold, silver, copper, and tin. Alaska is also one of the world's top producers of zinc concentrate. Fishing is another big business. Alaskan fishers produce more than 5 billion pounds (2.3 billon kilograms) of seafood each year.

A Changing Economy

Today, we know that using **fossil fuels** such as oil is harmful to the environment. Because of this, many people are searching for ways to use less oil. In addition, there has been an increase in competition from other energy sources in the country, such as wind and solar power. This has had a big effect on Alaska's economy. Since 1988, the state's oil production has decreased by 75 percent. This means there is less money flowing into the state. Because Alaska has much lower taxes than other states, it relies on income from oil to fund the government. Decreasing oil production also means fewer jobs in the oil industry. As the economy continues to change, Alaskans will continue to look elsewhere for income.

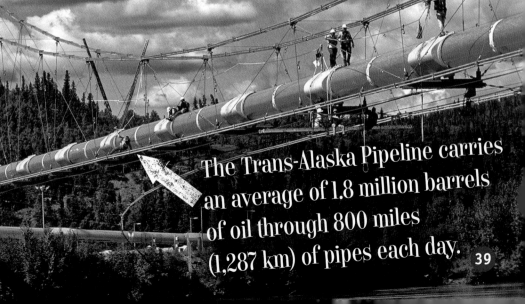

The Trans-Alaska Pipeline carries an average of 1.8 million barrels of oil through 800 miles (1,287 km) of pipes each day.

39

Eating in Alaska

Seafood is a big part of the local cuisine in Alaska. Freshly caught salmon and Alaskan king crab legs are local favorites.

Blueberries, cranberries, and strawberries all grow in the wild in Alaska. Some Native Alaskans combine them with animal fat or fish to make a unique style of ice cream.

 ## Alaskan Ice Cream

Ask an adult to help you!

Enjoy this delicious and easy-to-prepare dessert!

Ingredients
1 cup vegetable shortening
1 cup sugar
1/2 cup water, divided
4 cups mixed berries

Directions
Place the shortening in a pot over low heat. Stir until it melts to liquid. Add the sugar as you continue stirring. Once the sugar is completely melted, remove the pot from the heat. Keep stirring and add 1/4 cup of water. The mixture will start to cool and thicken. Add the rest of the water. Continue stirring until the mixture is fluffy and white. Now mix the berries in. Set the mixture in the freezer for at least one hour, and then enjoy!

The Last Frontier

With its remote location and strong native culture, Alaska is unlike anywhere else in the United States. Traveling to the Last Frontier isn't always easy, but as any resident will tell you, the experience of being there is well worth the effort. The stunning natural landscapes and the Alaskan way of life are a big part of the draw for residents and visitors alike. ★

Hikers stand atop a glacier at Wrangell–St. Elias National Park in south-central Alaska.

Famous People

Joseph Juneau

(1836–1899) was a Canadian miner who moved to Alaska during a gold rush in the late 1800s. He founded Alaska's capital city, Juneau, which is named for him.

Elizabeth Wanamaker Peratrovich

(1911–1958) was a Native Alaskan who fought discrimination against her people. Her efforts helped lead to the Alaska Anti-Discrimination Act of 1945.

William Egan

(1914–1984) served as Alaska's first governor. He is one of just two governors in Alaska's history to have been born in the state.

Libby Riddles

(1956–) is a dog musher who moved to Alaska as a teenager. In 1985, she made history by becoming the first woman to win the Iditarod.

Mary Youngblood

(1958–) is a Grammy-winning musician who is famous for performing traditional Native Alaskan music. She performs her instrumental compositions using a traditional style of flute.

Sarah Palin

(1964–) served as the governor of Alaska from 2006 to 2009. In 2008, she was the Republican nominee for vice president.

Dan Mintz

(1981–) is a comedian, actor, and writer who was born and raised in Anchorage. He is most famous for providing the voice of Tina Belcher on the popular animated show *Bob's Burgers*.

Jewel Kilcher

(1974–) is a Grammy-nominated singer-songwriter who has sold tens of millions of albums. She grew up in Alaska, where she learned to play guitar and got her start as a performer.

Did You Know That ...

Malaspina Glacier, the largest glacier in Alaska, covers about 1,500 square miles (3,885 sq km). That is larger than the entire state of Rhode Island!

Teachers from all over the country travel to Alaska's most remote, rural areas to teach children at "bush schools."

Ancient people in Alaska sometimes chopped down trees using beaver teeth.

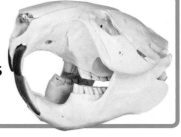

Alaska is home to 24 national park areas, covering 54,654,052 acres (22,117,710 ha), which is about 13 percent of the state.

In 1989, an oil tanker crashed into a reef in Alaska's Prince William Sound, releasing 11 million gallons (42 million liters) of oil into the water.

Because towns in Alaska are so spread out, about 1 in 58 of the state's people has a license to fly an airplane.

Alaskans have special names for different kinds of wind. A *chinook* is a warm wind in early spring or late winter. A *taku* is a cold, powerful arctic wind. A *williwaw* is a sudden, unexpected gust.

Did you find the truth?

(F) The United States purchased Alaska from Great Britain in 1867.

(T) There are parts of Alaska where the sun doesn't rise for up to 10 weeks at a time.

Resources

Books

Nonfiction

Cunningham, Kevin, and Peter Benoit. *The Inuit*. New York: Children's Press, 2011.

Orr, Tamra B. *Alaska*. New York: Children's Press, 2014.

Fiction

Hall, Elizabeth. *Child of the Wolves*. Boston: Houghton Mifflin, 1996.

London, Jack. *White Fang*. London: Methuen, 1907.

Morey, Walt. *Gentle Ben*. New York: Dutton, 1965.

Movies

Balto (1995)

The Big Year (2011)

The Gold Rush (1925)

Lost in Alaska (1952)

North to Alaska (1960)

Snow Buddies (2008)

Snow Dogs (2002)

White Fang (1991)

Visit this Scholastic website for more information on Alaska:
★ www.factsfornow.scholastic.com
Enter the keyword **Alaska**

Important Words

Arctic Circle (AHRK-tik SUR-kuhl) the line north of which the sun doesn't rise on the shortest day of the year or set on the longest day of the year

fossil fuels (FAH-suhl FYOOLZ) coal, oil, or natural gas, formed from the remains of prehistoric plants and animals

frontier (fruhn-TEER) the far edge of a country, where few people live

minerals (MIN-ur-uhlz) solid substances found in the earth that do not come from an animal or plant

peninsula (puh-NIN-suh-luh) a piece of land that sticks out from a larger landmass and is almost completely surrounded by water

permafrost (PUR-muh-frahst) land that has a permanently frozen layer of soil

territory (TER-uh-tor-ee) land controlled by a state

treaty (TREE-tee) a formal written agreement between two or more countries

tundra (TUHN-druh) a very cold area where there are no trees and the soil under the surface of the ground is always frozen

Index

Page numbers in **bold** indicate illustrations.

About the Author

Josh Gregory is the author of more than 100 books for kids. He has written about everything from animals to technology to history. A graduate of the University of Missouri–Columbia, he currently lives in Portland, Oregon.